I0811206

CORE LIBRARY OF US STATES

RHODE ISLAND

BY A. W. BUCKEY

CONTENT CONSULTANT
Geralyn Ducady, M.A.
Director of Education, Newell D. Goff Center for Education and Public Programs
State Coordinator, Rhode Island History Day
Rhode Island Historical Society

Core Library
An Imprint of Abdo Publishing
abdobooks.com

abdobooks.com

Published by Abdo Publishing, a division of ABDO, PO Box 398166, Minneapolis, Minnesota 55439.
Copyright © 2023 by Abdo Consulting Group, Inc. International copyrights reserved in all countries. No part of this book may be reproduced in any form without written permission from the publisher. Core Library™ is a trademark and logo of Abdo Publishing.

Printed in the United States of America, North Mankato, Minnesota.
052022
092022

THIS BOOK CONTAINS RECYCLED MATERIALS

Cover Photo: Shutterstock Images
Interior Photos: Denis Tangney Jr./Getty Images, 4–5; Red Line Editorial, 8 (Rhode Island), 8 (USA); Bettmann/Getty Images, 10–11, 43; North Wind Picture Archives/Alamy, 15; Shutterstock Images, 17 (flag), 17 (calamari), 17 (flower); Ariene Studio/Shutterstock Images, 17 (bird); Tatyana Mi/Shutterstock Images, 17 (tree); Arena Creative/Shutterstock Images, 20–21, 45; Gretchen Gunda Enger/Shutterstock Images, 24; Doug McGrady/Flickr, 26; Andrei Orlov/Alamy, 28–29; Carol M. Highsmith/Buyenlarge/Archive Photos/Getty Images, 31; Jay Yuan/Shutterstock Images, 33; Maddie Meyer/Getty Images Sport/Getty Images, 34–35; Jim Schubert/Shutterstock Images, 37; Robert K. Chin/Storefronts/Alamy, 40

Editor: Katharine Hale
Series Designer: Joshua Olson

Library of Congress Control Number: 2021951559

Publisher's Cataloging-in-Publication Data

Names: Buckey, A. W., author.
Title: Rhode Island / by A. W. Buckey
Description: Minneapolis, Minnesota : Abdo Publishing, 2023 | Series: Core library of US states | Includes online resources and index.
Identifiers: ISBN 9781532197819 (lib. bdg.) | ISBN 9781098270575 (ebook)
Subjects: LCSH: U.S. states--Juvenile literature. | Northeastern States--Juvenile literature. | Rhode Island--History--Juvenile literature. | Physical geography--United States--Juvenile literature.
Classification: DDC 974.5--dc23

Population demographics broken down by race and ethnicity come from the 2019 census estimate. Population totals come from the 2020 census.

CONTENTS

CHAPTER ONE

THE OCEAN STATE

It's easy to wake up early in Providence, Rhode Island. The city has more coffee and doughnut shops per person than any other city in the country. A delicious breakfast is close by, and there's plenty to see.

Providence is a city of art and experiments. It's home to a famous art college called the Rhode Island School of Design (RISD). Students there learn to become painters, sculptors, designers, and more. The RISD museum has artwork from around the world.

The Providence River runs through Providence.

PROVIDENCE DINERS

A diner is a type of inexpensive restaurant that often looks like a railroad car. Most diners serve a large all-day breakfast menu and are open late. The first diner opened in Providence. In 1872 a man named Walter Scott started a restaurant from his horse cart. He served Providence workers who had just finished their shifts.

Food is a big part of Providence's history and culture. People have been eating Rhode Island's famous clams and oysters for thousands of years. Today Providence has immigrants from all around the world. Each group has brought its food traditions to the city. The Federal Hill neighborhood is famous for Italian food. Broad Street has delicious Dominican restaurants. And Los Andes is known for South American dishes.

The Providence River runs right through the city. Summer and fall bring a special tradition. There are 100 floating metal torches on the river. Their fires light up the night. There is art, music, and food to enjoy. This tradition is called WaterFire. The Providence River runs into Narragansett Bay and the Atlantic Ocean. In Rhode Island, the ocean is always nearby.

EXPLORING RHODE ISLAND

Rhode Island is the smallest state in the United States. It is just 37 miles (60 km) wide and 48 miles (77 km) long. It's possible to drive across the whole state in just one hour. Rhode Island is not an island, but it has almost 400 miles (640 km) of shoreline. That's why Rhode Island is called the Ocean State.

Rhode Island is in the northeastern United States. It is part of a region called New England. The Atlantic

PERSPECTIVES

DIRT PALACE

Providence's nickname is the Creative Capital. Many artists are drawn to the city. There are organizations that help Providence artists succeed. Dirt Palace is a Providence space that supports female artists. Its mission is to help female artists change the world through their art. The space was founded in 2000 in an abandoned library building in Providence. Dirt Palace gives money, space, and resources to female artists. Local artists display their work in its gallery.

MAP OF RHODE ISLAND

Study the map below. What do you notice about the location of Rhode Island's cities? How does this map help you understand Rhode Island's unique geography?

Ocean borders Rhode Island to the south, and Connecticut lies to the west. Massachusetts makes up the northern and eastern borders of the state. Peoples such as the Niantic, Nipmuc, Narragansett, and Wampanoag have lived in the area for thousands of years. The state has a complex history. The founders of Rhode Island valued freedom and diversity. Rhode Island became wealthy from big businesses. But not everyone shared in this freedom and wealth. Today more than 1 million people call Rhode Island home. They come from many backgrounds and lead different lives. They share in the state's rich culture.

EXPLORE ONLINE

Chapter One discusses the state of Rhode Island. The article at the website below goes into more depth on this topic. Does the article answer any questions you have about Rhode Island?

RHODE ISLAND

abdocorelibrary.com/rhode-island

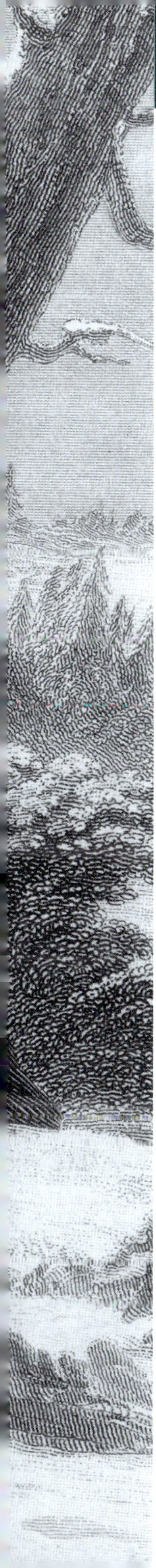

CHAPTER TWO

HISTORY OF RHODE ISLAND

People have been living in what is now Rhode Island for more than 10,000 years. The Wampanoag, Niantic, Nipmuc, and Narragansett peoples all came to live in the area. These peoples spoke similar languages.

By 1600 CE the Wampanoag people lived in the southeastern areas of modern day Rhode Island. They lived near the sea and on islands. The Nipmuc people lived in northwestern Rhode Island. The Eastern Niantic people

A historical illustration shows the Narragansett people helping Roger Williams after he was banished from Massachusetts.

lived in southwestern Rhode Island. The Narragansett were the largest nation in the area. They often provided protection to other smaller nations.

KING PHILIP'S WAR

King Philip's War (1675–1678) was a war between the Wampanoag and English colonists, with other American Indian peoples fighting on both sides. It is named after a Wampanoag sachem (leader) named Metacom. His nickname was King Philip. The Narragansett were originally neutral in this war. But the English worried they would join the Wampanoag. The English attacked a Narragansett settlement and killed hundreds of people. Most of the victims were women, children, and the elderly. This became known as the Great Swamp Massacre. The Narragansett then joined the Wampanoag. After the settlers were victorious, they sold many captured American Indians into slavery, even if they had not fought in the war.

EUROPEAN SETTLERS AND PROVIDENCE

When Europeans settled the area around Rhode Island after 1600, there were probably more than 100,000 American Indians there. The colonists brought contagious diseases such as smallpox to the area. American Indians had no resistance to these diseases. The diseases killed large numbers of American Indians.

Most of New England's European settlers were Puritans from England. They followed their own form of Protestant Christianity. They saw their settlements as colonies, or properties, of England. A man named Roger Williams moved from England to Massachusetts in 1630. After a few years, Williams clashed with the Massachusetts colony's leaders. Williams believed the church and the government should be separate. The colony banished Williams, and he started his own colony. He bought some land from the Narragansett people in 1636. Williams called the new colony Providence Plantations.

RHODE ISLAND IN THE EARLY UNITED STATES

Rhode Island was an early supporter of independence from British rule. But the Revolutionary War (1775–1783)

PERSPECTIVES

FIRST RHODE ISLAND REGIMENT

In 1778 Rhode Island was struggling to provide enough troops for the Revolutionary War. General James Varnum suggested that George Washington enlist enslaved people in Rhode Island. In February the Rhode Island Assembly voted to allow enslaved Black, mixed-race, and American Indian people to join the army. The law declared that "every slave so enlisting shall . . . be immediately discharged from the service of his [enslaver], and be absolutely free." Free and enslaved Black and American Indian men joined the First Rhode Island Regiment. They fought alongside white soldiers in the first official mixed-race regiment in the country.

was a difficult time for the colony. British forces occupied Newport for three years. British soldiers burned buildings for firewood. Eventually British soldiers left Newport for the South. The colonies eventually won the war and their independence from Britain. Rhode Island was the last of the 13 original colonies to ratify the US Constitution. It became a state in 1790.

Rhode Island relied on trade and

In 1772 Rhode Island colonists burned down a British ship called the *Gaspee*. They did this to protest British rule.

travel across the Atlantic Ocean. Providence, Bristol, and Newport were Rhode Island shore towns that ships could dock in. These towns became rich and powerful seaports. Rhode Islanders profited from the slave ships that came to the ports. The ships carried kidnapped African people who were sold into slavery in the United States and the Caribbean. Slavery was common in 1700s Rhode Island. However, the state passed the Gradual Emancipation Act in 1784. This was one of the first steps toward abolishing slavery in the state. Rhode Island banned the slave trade in 1787 and all slavery in 1843. But slavery was still allowed in other states. In 1861 the issue of slavery came to a head. Proslavery Southern states seceded from the United States. They created the Confederacy. The Northern states were known as the Union. Rhode Island was part of the antislavery Union. The American Civil War began in 1861 and ended with the Union's victory in 1865.

GROWTH, IMMIGRATION, AND MAJOR CHANGES

In the late 1700s through the 1800s, Rhode Island was a manufacturing center. Manufacturing is the process of making goods. The Industrial Revolution changed the manufacturing process in the 1800s. Before this time, items such as silverware, furniture, and cloth were made by hand. But in the 1800s, new machines made manufacturing faster and easier. Business owners built many mills and factories in Rhode Island. The state was especially known for cloth manufacturing. The first US cloth mill opened in Rhode Island in 1793.

RHODE ISLAND
QUICK FACTS

Each US state has its own unique history and culture. How do Rhode Island's state nickname and motto represent its history? Did you find any of Rhode Island's state symbols surprising?

Abbreviation: RI
Nickname: The Ocean State
Motto: Hope
Date of statehood: May 29, 1790
Capital: Providence
Population: 1,097,379
Area: 1,545 square miles (4,002 sq km)

STATE SYMBOLS

State appetizer
Calamari

State flower
Violet

State bird
Rhode Island Red

State tree
Red maple

Mill jobs were often dangerous, and they paid poorly. But there were a lot of opportunities to work. In the 1800s many Irish and French Canadian people came to work in Rhode Island. Later, Italian and Portuguese immigrants settled in the state. Immigrants from Central and South America, Asia, and Eastern Europe also came to Rhode Island. By 1910 about two-thirds of Rhode Islanders were immigrants or children of immigrants.

A small number of people got rich from the Industrial Revolution. In the late 1800s, famous American businessmen such as Cornelius Vanderbilt and J. P. Morgan made huge fortunes. These tycoons and their families chose Newport as their summer vacation spot. They built seaside mansions. Newport became famous as a symbol of American wealth.

GOVERNMENT

Rhode Island's government consists of three branches. The executive branch is made up of state leaders, including the governor. State senators and representatives meet in the General Assembly to make laws. They form the legislative branch. The judicial branch is the court system.

The Narragansett Indian Tribe is the only federally recognized American Indian tribe in Rhode Island. There are about 4,500 Narragansett people alive today. By the end of the 1800s, the US government had taken nearly all Narragansett lands. The Narragansett won back 1,800 acres (730 ha) of land in 1978. Today the tribal government headquarters is in Charlestown.

FURTHER EVIDENCE

Chapter Two discusses the history of Rhode Island, including the Industrial Revolution. What was one of the author's main points? What key evidence supports this point? Read the article at the website below. Does the information on the website support the information from the chapter? Does it present new evidence?

WHAT WAS THE INDUSTRIAL REVOLUTION?

abdocorelibrary.com/rhode-island

CHAPTER THREE

GEOGRAPHY AND CLIMATE

Like much of the northeastern United States, Rhode Island has a humid continental climate. This means that the summers are hot, and the winters are cold. Weather in Rhode Island changes a lot from day to day and from year to year. The state's closeness to the sea affects its climate. Near the ocean, winter tends to be warmer and summer cooler than in inland areas. This is because large bodies of water trap heat.

The Mohegan Bluffs on Block Island overlook the Atlantic Ocean.

Rhode Island includes several islands off the coast. To the south is Block Island. There are between 30 and 40 islands in Narragansett Bay. The biggest and most famous is Aquidneck Island. The city of Newport is there.

QUAHOG

A quahog (pronounced KOH-hawg) is a type of hard-shelled clam. These clams are native to the Atlantic coast. The name *quahog* comes from the Narragansett word *poquaûhock*. American Indian peoples including the Narragansett make wampum jewelry from quahog shells. Quahogs are especially easy to find in Rhode Island. They have become a big part of the state's traditional food. Rhode Island has Quahog Week every May, when restaurants cook special quahog dishes. One of the most famous quahog recipes is stuffies, or stuffed clams. The quahog is also the state shell of Rhode Island.

PLANTS, WILDLIFE, AND OCEAN LIFE

Rhode Island hosts many different ecosystems. Each has its own plants and wildlife. The forests of Rhode Island are home to mammals such as deer, foxes, rabbits, and a few black bears.

Newts and turtles live under rotting wood on the forest floor. Hundreds of bird species live in Rhode Island at least part of the year. Many birds nest and eat in the forests too.

Ocean life is a big part of Rhode Island's ecosystem. Several whale species travel through the oceans near the state. Beachgoers might see seals on the shore and dolphins and porpoises in the water. Shorebirds such as seagulls and

PERSPECTIVES

FISHING AND WIND FARMS

A wind farm is a way of collecting energy for electricity. Wind turns a large turbine, which looks like a giant fan. The energy from the turbine's rotation powers a generator and creates electricity. Wind energy has advantages. It does not pollute, and wind never runs out. Rhode Island built the first offshore wind farm in the United States in 2016. In 2021 businesspeople planned another Rhode Island wind farm. But some people said that the proposed wind farm would ruin an important fish habitat. It would also hurt the fishing business. The company agreed to use fewer wind turbines as a compromise.

Animals and people alike enjoy eating Rhode Island's quahogs.

terns live on the coast. And humans fish along the coastline. People harvest clams and oysters by digging for them in the sand. They can find squid, lobsters, sea bass, scallops, and tuna in the sea.

Rhode Island is one of the most densely populated states in the country. This means that in some places, there are a lot of people living together in a small area. Some wildlife species end up living among humans. Raccoons and skunks, for example, show up often in Rhode Island cities and towns. In addition, humans sometimes introduce plants and animals from elsewhere. These nonnative species can disrupt the natural environment. When they do, they're called invasive species. Rhode Island's invasive species include the European green crab and the Asian shore crab.

CONSERVATION IN RHODE ISLAND

Rhode Islanders work to protect wildlife and plants. People in the state have replanted a lot of trees in the last few hundred years. Today more than 60 percent of the state's land is forested. The state controls hunting and fishing by selling licenses. The licenses control the number and type of animals killed each year. Money from the licenses pays for conservation programs. State parks, beaches, and management areas help preserve Rhode Island's natural beauty. Arcadia Management Area is the largest recreational area in the state.

The drumheads milkwort is a plant native to Rhode Island. It is found in wet and coastal areas.

It covers 14,000 acres (5,700 ha) of forested land. Other state lands include the Buck Hill Management Area and George Washington Management Area.

Nonprofit groups also help conserve nature. The Rhode Island Wild Plant Society is an organization that works to protect native plants. These are plants that existed before Europeans came to the state. Native plants help reduce pollution, feed wildlife, and keep ecosystems healthy.

STRAIGHT TO THE SOURCE

In 2020 the COVID-19 pandemic led to shutdowns throughout the United States. People had to stay away from each other to prevent spreading a contagious virus. Jay Osenkowski is the deputy chief of the Rhode Island Department of Environmental Management Division of Fish and Wildlife. He said:

> *At the Rhode Island Division of Fish & Wildlife, resiliency and innovation were the key to success during this difficult year. . . .*
>
> *Rhode Islanders flocked to State Management Areas to seek refuge from long days inside, further strengthening our need for wild spaces. . . .*
>
> *This year proved that when all else fails, we turn to nature. This truth is what fuels us to protect, conserve and restore Rhode Island's natural resources now and for generations to come.*

Source: *Division of Fish and Wildlife: Annual Wildlife Report 2020.* Rhode Island Department of Environmental Management, n.d., dem.ri.gov. PDF. Accessed 11 Oct. 2021.

WHAT'S THE BIG IDEA?

Take a close look at this passage. What is the main point Osenkowski is making? What can you tell about his views on conservation from the passage?

FURUNO

CHAPTER FOUR

RESOURCES AND ECONOMY

Oceans still play a big role in Rhode Island's economy and resources. Ships are built and docked in Rhode Island. The state is a beach vacation destination. But the state's economy looks different than it did in the past. At the beginning of the 1900s, 60 percent of Rhode Islanders worked in manufacturing. Fewer than 16 percent did 100 years later. Today more Rhode Islanders make money in service-based jobs. They do important tasks for other people.

Fishing is a major industry in Rhode Island.

WHERE RHODE ISLANDERS WORK

The biggest industries in Rhode Island are health care; retail and service; and professional, scientific, and technical services. Doctors, nurses, pharmacists, and nursing-home staff are parts of the health-care industry. They treat diseases and take care of sick people. Service employees help with the tasks of daily life. Common service positions include restaurant staff and hotel employees. Retail workers are service employees who sell things in stores.

People working in professional, scientific, and technical services have a wide variety of jobs. These workers

SQUID FISHING IN RHODE ISLAND

The oceans off the coast of Rhode Island are home to many species of squid. Longfin inshore squid are used in the popular dish calamari. Rhode Island squid fishers catch more than half of the calamari squid harvested in the northeastern United States. In 2020 they caught more than 20 million pounds (9.1 million kg) of squid. Rhode Island fishers sell their squid across the country and world.

The US Naval War College was founded in 1884.

train to get a special skill. They are lawyers, photographers, researchers, architects, and more.

The US Navy has several operations in Rhode Island. The navy does a lot of education and training in Newport. The US Naval War College is there. Newport also has a naval station. The navy uses the station to test new equipment.

PERSPECTIVES

JEWELRY MAKING IN RHODE ISLAND

In the 1900s Rhode Island was nicknamed the jewelry capital of the world. The jewelry industry declined in the late 1900s. But some people are working to revive it in the state. Rhode Island still has the factories and equipment the industry needs. There are even Rhode Island warehouses full of untouched crystals and beads. Famous jewelry brands such as Tiffany & Co. and Alex and Ani use manufacturers in the state. Rhode Islander Carolyn Rafaelian founded Alex and Ani. She said, "Here comes a company that has never left the state. Even the paper we use has to be made here. . . . I love the state so much and it has an amazing amount of potential."

EDUCATION AND TOURISM

Rhode Island is known for its many colleges and universities. Most of these schools are in Providence. The Rhode Island School of Design and Brown University are the most famous. Brown is one of the eight Ivy League colleges and universities. The Ivy League schools are extremely selective and are known for their successful graduates. Johnson and Wales University is another

Rhode Island's beaches attract tourists.

top-ranked Rhode Island college. This school is known for culinary arts.

Summer tourism is a big part of Rhode Island's economy. People come from all over to enjoy the Ocean State. When people visit the state, they stay at hotels and take ferries. They eat at restaurants or try kayaking and surfing. They might buy new swimsuits and shop for souvenirs. People in service jobs make all these things possible. Approximately 13 percent of jobs in Rhode Island are related to tourism or travel.

CHAPTER FIVE

PEOPLE AND PLACES

Approximately 1 million people live in Rhode Island. White people who are not Hispanic or Latino make up 71 percent of Rhode Island's population. Today about one in five Rhode Islanders is Italian American. In fact, Rhode Island has the largest percentage of Italian Americans of any US state. People of many other heritages also call the state home. Approximately 16 percent of Rhode Islanders are Hispanic or Latino. Spanish is the

Newport, Rhode Island, is home to the first US polo club.

second-most spoken language in the state. Black Rhode Islanders make up 8.5 percent of the state's population. There are large Black communities in Providence and surrounding towns such as Pawtucket and Central Falls. Approximately 4 percent of Rhode Islanders are Asian, and 1 percent are American Indian.

VIOLA DAVIS

Viola Davis is a theater, film, and TV actor. She is the first Black woman to have won a Tony, an Emmy, and an Oscar. These are the three major acting awards in the United States. Davis was born in South Carolina in 1965 but grew up in Central Falls, Rhode Island. She started acting in high school and at Rhode Island College. Davis returns to Rhode Island often. She grew up in poverty and wants to help struggling Rhode Islanders. In 2017 she went to her hometown to support a new health clinic. In 2020 Davis donated $10,000 to her old high school's theater program.

CITIES AND DESTINATIONS

Providence is Rhode Island's biggest and most diverse city. It's the go-to destination for the arts. But many Rhode Island destinations

Castle Hill is a lighthouse in Newport.

are outside the city limits. For example, Block Island is famous for its beaches and boating. The island is 13 miles (21 km) off the US coast. Block Island treasures its small community and natural beauty. About half the island's land is protected from construction.

Rhode Island has beaches for people with all kinds of interests. Goosewing Beach Preserve is a protected area and home to two rare bird species. Oakland Beach in Warwick has a boardwalk for walks and shopping. Narragansett Beach is popular with surfers. People who love lighthouses can visit Warwick, Wakefield, and Newport harbors.

SPORTS

Rhode Island's only professional sports team is the Providence Bruins hockey team. But other sports are important in the state's culture. In the late 1800s, millionaires came to Newport to relax and have fun. They brought summer sports and entertainment with them. In 1895 the first US Open golf tournament took place in Newport. Today the area has several well-known golf courses. The America's Cup race is an international yachting race held since 1851. Newport hosted the event 12 times between 1930 and 1983. The race was also held in Newport in 2012.

Tennis was popular in historic Newport. The first US men's tennis championship took place there in 1880. Newport is now home to the International Tennis Hall of Fame. People can play tennis inside and outside the Hall of Fame building.

The first US polo club was also in Newport. Polo is an ancient sport with roots in Asia. It is played a little like field hockey but on horseback. Since each polo player must have a horse, the game is very expensive. Newport was a natural place for polo to thrive. The Newport Polo Club still hosts polo matches and tournaments. Anyone can buy tickets to watch the fast-paced play.

PERSPECTIVES

RHODE ISLAND ACCENT

The Rhode Island accent is a type of New England accent. People with this accent do not pronounce the *r* sound in some words. For example, "I park my car" might sound like "I pawk my caw." They may also add an *r* sound to the ends of some words. For example, "idea" might sound like "idear." This accent originally comes from English settlers. Italian and Irish immigrants also influenced the Rhode Island accent. Rhode Islanders have their own slang words too. For example, milkshakes are "cabinets" and drinking fountains are "bubblers."

RHODE ISLAND CULTURE

Rhode Island has some unique food traditions. The state even has an

Olneyville New York System is a famous hot wiener restaurant in Providence.

official drink, called coffee milk. It's made by mixing cold milk with coffee syrup. In Rhode Island, coffee milk is as common as chocolate milk. Kids drink it at school, and grocery stores sell it. The hot wiener is another Rhode Island staple. It's a hot dog with meat sauce, onion, celery salt, and mustard. Calamari, or fried squid rings, is the Rhode Island state appetizer. Rhode Island–style calamari is served with hot peppers. The state's unique foods blend American Indian ingredients and influences with the cultures of many waves of immigrants and settlers. Rhode Island food is like the state itself. Both are part of the American story, but with a spirit and history of their own.

STRAIGHT TO THE SOURCE

Previously, Rhode Island's official name was The State of Rhode Island and Providence Plantations. In 2020 Rhode Islanders voted to remove "and Providence Plantations." A petition explained the importance of the name change:

> *The addition of "and Providence Plantations" happened in 1644 after the colonial merger of Providence, Portsmouth, Newport, and Warwick. Roger Williams had intended "Plantation" to mean colony or settlement, but the modern connotation of that word has changed. If you ask anyone what's the first word that comes to your mind when you [hear] plantation? They'll likely say slavery, and to every African American it holds a painful memory and represents the very real systematic racism in our government.*

Source: Tyson Pianka, "Change the Official Name of Rhode Island." *Change.org*, 2019, change.org. Accessed 1 Sept. 2021.

CONSIDER YOUR AUDIENCE

Adapt this passage for a different audience, such as your principal or friends. Write a blog post conveying this same information to the new audience. How does your post differ from the original text and why?

IMPORTANT DATES

More than 10,000 years ago
The first inhabitants live in what is now Rhode Island.

1636 CE
Roger Williams founds Providence Plantations.

1775
The Revolutionary War begins.

1787
Rhode Island outlaws the slave trade.

1790
Rhode Island becomes a state.

1800s
Manufacturing in Rhode Island attracts thousands of immigrants.

1843
Rhode Island bans slavery.

1880

The first men's national tennis championship takes place in Newport.

2020

Rhode Island changes its official name from The State of Rhode Island and Providence Plantations to simply Rhode Island.

STOP AND THINK

You Are There

This book discusses Rhode Island's beaches. Imagine you are visiting the Rhode Island shore. Write a letter home telling your friends about what you have found. What plants and animals do you see? Be sure to add plenty of detail to your notes.

Surprise Me

Chapter Two discusses Rhode Island's history. After reading this book, what two or three facts about the history of the state did you find most surprising? Write a few sentences about each fact. Why did you find each fact surprising?

Take a Stand

Rhode Island is known for its food traditions. Imagine a friend or family member wanted to try one of Rhode Island's unique foods or drinks. Which would you recommend trying and why?

Another View

This book talks about the Industrial Revolution. As you know, every source is different. Ask a librarian or another adult to help you find another source about this topic. Write a short essay comparing and contrasting the new source's point of view with that of this book's author. What is the point of view of each author? How are they similar and why? How are they different and why?

GLOSSARY

conservation
the act of protecting plants and animals

culinary arts
arts and skills related to cooking and serving food

ecosystem
a community of living things, together with their environment

habitat
the place where a plant or an animal lives

humid
having a lot of moisture in the air

immigrant
a person who moves to and lives in a new country

industry
a type of business or job

plantation
a large farm where the workers live on-site

ratify
to sign or give formal consent to an agreement or document

resiliency
the ability to adjust to or recover from change

tycoon
a very rich and powerful businessperson

ONLINE RESOURCES

To learn more about Rhode Island, visit our free resource websites below.

Core Library CONNECTION
FREE! COMMON CORE MULTIMEDIA RESOURCES

Visit **abdocorelibrary.com** or scan this QR code for free Common Core resources for teachers and students, including vetted activities, multimedia, and booklinks, for deeper subject comprehension.

Booklinks NONFICTION NETWORK
FREE! ONLINE NONFICTION RESOURCES

Visit **abdobooklinks.com** or scan this QR code for free additional online weblinks for further learning. These links are routinely monitored and updated to provide the most current information available.

LEARN MORE

Lusted, Marcia Amidon. *Intro to Horse Polo*. Abdo, 2018.

Schumacher, Cassandra. *Rhode Island*. Cavendish Square, 2020.

INDEX

About the Author

A. W. Buckey is a writer living in Brooklyn, New York. She is going to learn how to make coffee milk.